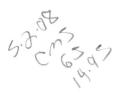

D0125087

WEEKLY **WR** READER
EARLY LEARNING LIBRARY

Let's Read About Dinosaurs

Apatosaurus

by Joanne Mattern
Illustrations by Jeffrey Magniat

Reading consultant: Susan Nations, M.Ed., author/literacy coach/
consultant in literacy development

Science consultant: Philip J. Currie, Ph.D., Professor and Canada Research
Chair of Dinosaur Palaeobiology at the University of Alberta, Canada

Please visit our web site at: www.garethstevens.com
For a free color catalog describing Weekly Reader® Early Learning Library's
list of high-quality books, call 1-800-542-2595 (USA) or 1-800-387-3178 (Canada).
Gareth Stevens Publishing's fax: (877) 542-2596

Library of Congress Cataloging-in-Publication Data

Mattern, Joanne, 1963-
 Apatosaurus / by Joanne Mattern.
  p. cm. — (Let's read about dinosaurs)
 Includes bibliographical references and index.
 ISBN-10: 0-8368-7695-4   ISBN-13: 978-0-8368-7695-6 (lib. bdg.)
 ISBN-10: 0-8368-7702-0   ISBN-13: 978-0-8368-7702-1 (softcover)
 1. Apatosaurus—Juvenile literature. I. Title.
 QE862.S3M332   2007
 567.913'8—dc22   2006029970

This edition first published in 2007 by
Weekly Reader® Early Learning Library
An Imprint of Gareth Stevens Publishing
1 Reader's Digest Rd.
Pleasantville, NY 10570-7000 USA

Copyright © 2007 by Weekly Reader® Early Learning Library

Managing editor: Valerie J. Weber
Art direction, cover and layout design: Tammy West

Printed in the United States of America

2 3 4 5 6 7 8 9 10 10 09 08 07

Note to Educators and Parents

Reading is such an exciting adventure for young children! They are beginning to integrate their oral language skills with written language. To encourage children along the path to early literacy, books must be colorful, engaging, and interesting; they should invite the young reader to explore both the print and the pictures.

Let's Read about Dinosaurs is a new series designed to help children read about some of their favorite — and most fearsome — animals. In each book, young readers will learn how each dinosaur survived so long ago.

Each book is specially designed to support the young reader in the reading process. The familiar topics are appealing to young children and invite them to read — and re-read — again and again. The full-color photographs and enhanced text further support the student during the reading process.

In addition to serving as wonderful picture books in schools, libraries, homes, and other places where children learn to love reading, these books are specifically intended to be read within an instructional guided reading group. This small group setting allows beginning readers to work with a fluent adult model as they make meaning from the text. After children develop fluency with the text and content, the book can be read independently. Children and adults alike will find these books supportive, engaging, and fun!

— Susan Nations, M.Ed., author, literacy coach,
and consultant in literacy development

Dinosaurs lived on Earth millions of years ago. One of the largest dinosaurs was Apatosaurus (uh-pa-tuh-SAWR-us).

Apatosaurus was as long as four big trucks lined up! Apatosaurus weighed as much as thirty-six cars!

Apatosaurus had a long neck. It had a big, heavy body. Its tail was very long.

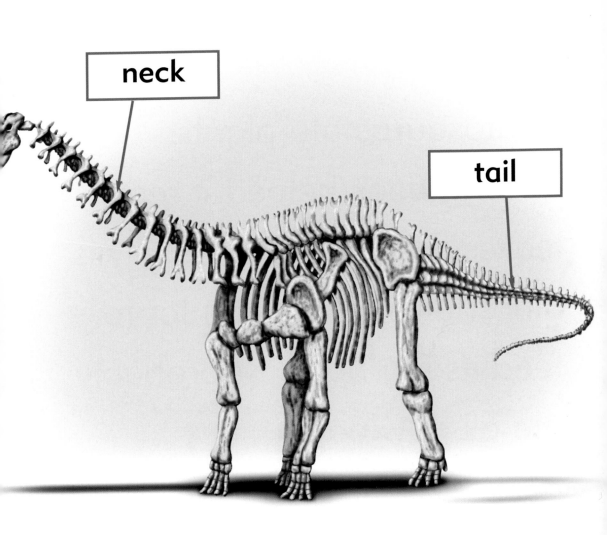

neck

tail

9

Apatosaurus ate plants.
Its long neck helped it reach
leaves high in the trees. This
dinosaur had to eat a lot to
feed its big body. It probably
ate all day long.

Apatosaurus also ate stones!
The stones helped the
dinosaur digest its food.

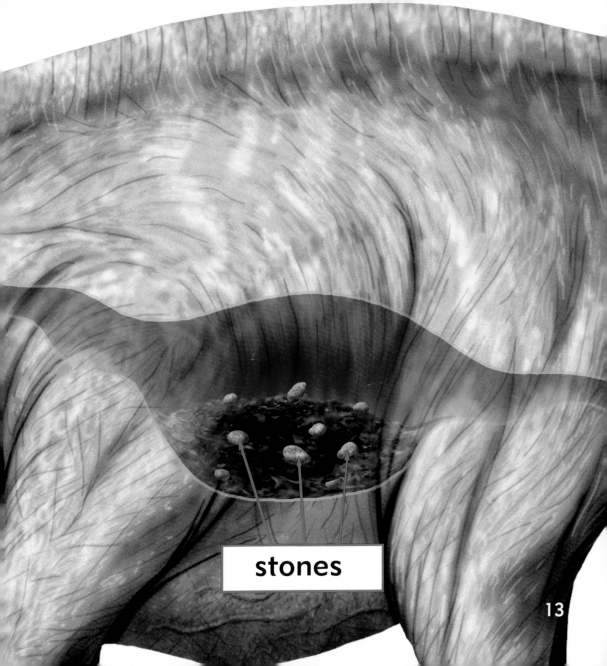

stones

Some dinosaurs liked to eat Apatosaurus. Dinosaurs that ate other dinosaurs are called **predators**.

Apatosaurus had a way to stay safe from predators. They lived in large groups called **herds**. It was hard for a predator to attack many Apatosaurus at the same time.

Apatosaurus laid eggs. An Apatosaurus egg could be a foot wide! A baby Apatosaurus could take care of itself as soon as it was born.

Apatosaurus died out a long time ago. However, many dinosaur museums show Apatosaurus bones. It is fun to see this giant that walked the Earth so long ago.

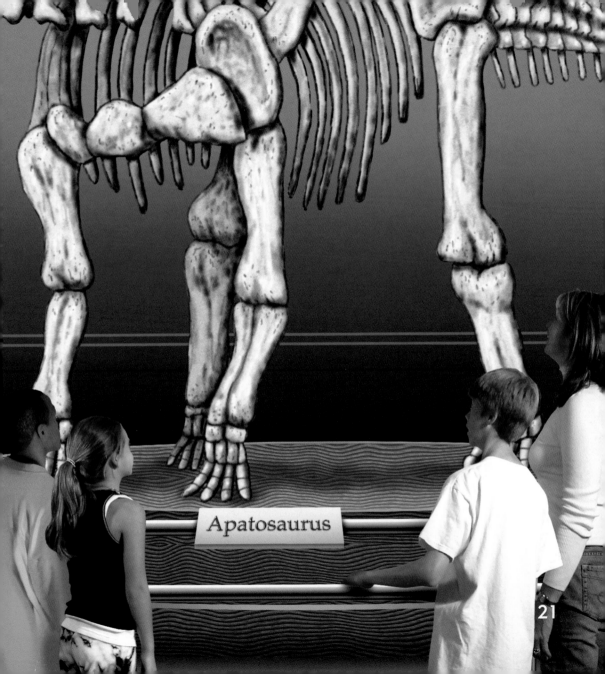

Apatosaurus

21

Glossary

digest — to break down food

herds — large groups of animals

museums — a place where interesting objects are shown to the public

predators — animals that eat other animals

For More Information

Books

Apatosaurus. Dinosaurs Set I (series).
Richard Gaines (Buddy Books)

Apatosaurus. Discovering Dinosaurs (series).
Daniel Cohen (Bridgestone Books)

Apatosaurus. Science of Dinosaurs (series).
Susan Heinrichs Gray (Child's World)

Web Site

Apatosaurus

www.enchantedlearning.com/subjects/dinosaurs/dinos/
Apatosaurus.shtml

This Web site has facts, drawings, and charts about
Apatosaurus, plus links to other dinosaur sites.

Publisher's note to educators and parents: Our editors have carefully reviewed this Web site to ensure that it is suitable for children. Many Web sites change frequently, however, and we cannot guarantee that a site's future contents will continue to meet our high standards of quality and educational value. Be advised that children should be closely supervised whenever they access the Internet.

Index

About the Author

Joanne Mattern has written more than 150 books for children. She has written about weird animals, sports, world cities, dinosaurs, and many other subjects. Joanne also works in her local library. She lives in New York State with her husband, three daughters, and assorted pets. She enjoys animals, music, going to baseball games, reading, and visiting schools to talk about her books.

24